PUFFIN BOOKS

You Wait Till I'm Older Than You

Michael Rosen was brought up in London. He originally tried to study medicine before starting to write poems and stories. His poems are about all kinds of things – but always important things – from chocolate cake to bathtime. In 2007, Michael was appointed the fifth Children's Laureate – a role he decided would be used to be an 'ambassador of fun'.

michaelrosen.co.uk

D0993560

Books by Michael Rosen

CENTRALLY HEATED KNICKERS
MICHAEL ROSEN'S BOOK OF VERY SILLY
POEMS (Ed.)
NO BREATHING IN CLASS (with Korky Paul)
QUICK, LET'S GET OUT OF HERE
YOU WAIT TILL I'M OLDER THAN YOU!

You Wait Till I'm Older Than You

Hilarious poems by
Michael ROSEN

Illustrated by Shoo Rayner

PUFFIN

PUFFIN BOOKS

Published by the Penguin Group
Penguin Books Ltd, 80 Strand, London WC2R 0RL, England
Penguin Group (USA) Inc., 375 Hudson Street, New York, New York 10014, USA
Penguin Group (Canada), 90 Eglinton Avenue East, Suite 700, Toronto, Ontario, Canada M4P 2Y3
(a division of Pearson Penguin Canada Inc.)
Penguin Ireland, 25 St Stephen's Green, Dublin 2, Ireland (a division of Penguin Books Ltd)
Penguin Group (Australia), 250 Camberwell Road, Camberwell, Victoria 3124, Australia
(a division of Pearson Australia Group Pty Ltd)
Penguin Books India Pvt Ltd, 11 Community Centre, Panchsheel Park, New Delhi – 110 017, India
Penguin Group (NZ), 67 Apollo Drive, Rosedale, North Shore 0632, New Zealand
(a division of Pearson New Zealand Ltd)
Penguin Books (South Africa) (Pty) Ltd, 24 Sturdee Avenue, Rosebank, Johannesburg 2196, South Africa

Penguin Books Ltd, Registered Offices: 80 Strand, London WC2R 0RL, England

puffinbooks.com

First published by Viking Books 1996
Published in Puffin Books 1997
23

Text copyright © Michael Rosen, 1996
Illustrations copyright © Shoo Rayner, 1996
All rights reserved

The moral right of the author and illustrator has been asserted

Set in Baskerville
Made and printed in England by Clays Ltd, St Ives plc

British Library Cataloguing in Publication Data
A CIP catalogue record for this book is available from the British Library

ISBN: 978-0-140-38014-9

www.greenpenguin.co.uk

Mixed Sources
Product group from well-managed
forests and other controlled sources
www.fsc.org Cert no. SA-COC-1592
© 1996 Forest Stewardship Council

Penguin Books is committed to a sustainable future
for our business, our readers and our planet.
The book in your hands is made from paper
certified by the Forest Stewardship Council.

Contents

Who Started It?

When me and my brother have a fight
my mum says:
'Stoppit – someone'll get hurt.'

And we say:
'He started it.'
'I didn't. He started it.'

I say:
'Mum, who started the very first fight
between me and Brian?'

And she says:
'You.'

'Me? But I'm four years younger than him.
How could it have been me?'

And she says:
'Well, it was like this . . .

You were about two years old
and Brian was six.
You were sitting in your high chair
eating your breakfast
and Brian walked past.
You leaned forward
and banged him over the head
with your spoon.'

'There you are,' says my brother,
'you started it,
you started it.
I always knew you started it.'

Useful Instructions

Wipe that face off your smile
Don't eat with your mouthful
When you cough, put your ear over your mouth
Don't bite your nose
Don't talk while I'm interrupting
How many tunes do I have to tell you?!

Running

Above the tap it said
'Run a long time
to get hot water.'

So I ran round the room for a really long time
but I didn't get any hot water.

Stealing

Harrybo says:
'That's the best toy car you've nicked yet,
it's –'
My dad walks in behind him.
'What did you just say, Harrybo?'

Great! He didn't hear Harrybo properly.

Harrybo turns round –
' . . . about the car – the – er . . .'
'What car?'

Oh no! The questioning.

'Whose car is it?'
Together we say:
'It's Harrybo's.' 'It's Michael's.'
'Where's it from?'
'Woollies.'
'So who paid for it?'
Together we say:
'Him.' 'Him.'
'It couldn't have been you, Michael,
you haven't got any money.
Where did you get the money from, Harrybo?'
'I didn't have the – er actually . . .'

It's all just about to blow up.

'Look, tell me if I got this wrong:
did I or did I not hear Harrybo say:
"It's the best toy car you've nicked yet"?'

There's no escape.

'Yiss.'
'What do you think Harrybo meant
when he said that?'

Play dumb.

'I'm not really sure.'
'Harrybo, what did you mean
when you said:
"It's the best toy car you've nicked yet"?'
Silence.
'Do you think Michael nicked the car?'
'Oh no. I wouldn't think he'd do a thing like that.'

Fool, Harrybo. He'll pounce on that.

'See, Michael, even your best friend . . .'

My best friend!

'. . . thinks you're not the sort of person
who'd do a thing like that.
Aren't you really sick of yourself?'

Course Harrybo doesn't think that.
He's got a Bluebird racing car
that he nicked as well
in his trouser pocket.

'Yiss.'
'Well, you know what you're going to do,
don't you?'
'Yiss.'
'What?'
'Take it back.'
'Exactly. And when you get back here
you, me and your mother
are going to have a long talk about this,
aren't we?'

I thought we just had.

'Aren't we?'
'Yiss.'

Raw Food

Harrybo's dad grows hundreds of vegetables
and Harrybo says:
'Let's go down the garden . . .'
and he attacks his dad's broad beans.
'Come on, you have some,' he says,
and he's munching through five of them.
I don't like them very much.
Maybe I'll just have one
to show I'm not feeble.

Then he goes for the peas.
'These are GREAT,' he says,
'really sweet.'
And he sticks his thumb in the pod
and squirts a row of raw peas into his mouth.

Sometimes he pulls up radishes and carrots,
wipes the mud off them
bites the tops off
and munches up the rest.

'You want to try potatoes, Michael,' he says,
and he heaves one of his dad's potatoes up,
wipes the mud off that too
and –
crunch –
he eats a raw potato
then
red currants
black currants
gooseberries.

I once said the red currants
smelt like cat's pee.
Didn't bother him.
He gobbles these till his chin
runs red.

And the apples.
His dad grows the hardest, bitterest apples
you've ever seen,
with knobbly, leathery skins.

'Great!' says Harrybo,
'let's get at the apples.'
And he munches them up:
the whole thing –
the core
the pips
the little hairy bits at the ends.
He leaves nothing.

He even found some little green pip things.
'Stursham seeds', he called them.
'Try these,' he says.
They were sour, peppery beans.
Horrible.
'I love these,' he said
and he scooped handfuls of them into his mouth.

It's incredible watching him
roaming round the garden
grabbing at anything growing.
He chews grass.
He eats dandelion leaves.
'These are just great, Michael,' he says.
'*You* ought to eat them, you know.'

I've seen people very carefully nibbling at
one raw mushroom
thinking they're doing something
daringly healthy.

Harrybo can munch up twenty.

The Deal

My brother once told me that
Mum and Dad have got a deal about
telling off.

He said that
if one of *them*
is telling one of *us* off
then the other parent
won't join in.
He said that they'd said
it isn't fair on a kid
if both parents have a go
at the same time.

It works like that most of the time.

My dad gets angry about something,
like the time I stuck toothpaste
in his shaving soap:
'What did you think?
I wouldn't notice?
The little fool!
He spends hours and hours in that bathroom
and we think he's washing himself!
But this is the sort of monkey business
he's getting up to.
This is my shaving soap.
Not yours.
If you want to play about with shaving soap
buy your own.'

And Mum doesn't say a word.
Not a word.

But somehow when it's Mum's turn
it doesn't quite work out the same way.

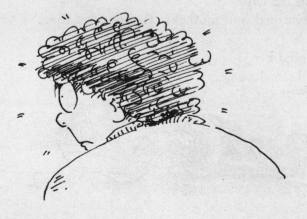

She's telling me off
for not cleaning my shoes:
'How can you go out like that?
You look like a tramp.
I don't want to be seen in the street with you.
All I'm asking is that you give them a wipe.
A little wipe.
That wouldn't harm you, would it?'

And out of the corner of my eye
I can see my dad
twitching about
itching to join in.
He's nodding and tutting
and coming in with:
'Quite!'
and
'You're right there, Connie.'

Then when Mum goes out the room
he bursts out with:
'You've pushed your mother to the edge this time.'

Never mind her,
he's well *over* the edge.

Harrybo

People often say to me
'What's become of Harrybo,
the boy in your poems?'

And I say:
'When I was 11
we had to do an exam
called the 11-plus.
I passed and went to a Grammar School.
Harrybo failed
and went to a Secondary Modern School.

So though up till then
we used to see each other every day
– weekends as well –
after that,
we didn't see much of each other at all.
I'd see him from the bus
talking with his new friends
and I was with mine.
One time when we met
he told me that once
him and his girlfriend were snogging
in his front room
and his mum was looking in
through the window.
It sounded very different from exploring
the ponds
and making go-karts.

When I was 17
we moved
and I didn't see him again.

When I was 38
I visited my old school
and a boy said his dad knew me
from when we were children
and he would like me to come back
for tea at his place.

When I got there
I found out it was Jimmy.
Giggly Jimmy, who hopped about on one foot
if he thought something was funny.
He's a truck driver now.
Jimmy said:
'Harrybo died when he was 17.
I don't know where his parents are.
They moved.'

Before Jimmy told me this
I had sometimes wondered
if somewhere some time
Harrybo had read all these things
I've been writing about him . . .
but he hadn't.

Calculator

If you turn a calculator upside down
you can make the numbers look like letters.

4 is h
3 is E
7 is L
8 is B
5 is S
6 is g
O is O
1 is l
2 is Z

so type in
8075 07734
turn the calculator round and you've got
hELLO SLOB

you can type in:

BOB gOBBLES BOILS
BOB glggLES
LIZZIE gOBBLES OIL
LIZZIE SIZZLES

BOB gOggLES
Oh BOSh BOB
hE SLOgS
gO gOB

15

Hospital

There's a boy on the other side of the ward
and his face is completely covered in plaster.

There's a man called Charlie
and his face has been burnt off.
He's got no face.
He shows me a picture of himself
before his accident.
He used to look like Elvis Presley.

The nurse says:
'When you go into the operating theatre
they're going to bang your nose straight
with a rubber hammer.'

I'm here because I was hit by a cricket ball.
I fell to the ground and shooting pains
went into my eyes.
The teacher rushed over and said:
'Did you catch it?'

My mother has a shiny dent in her nose
with a little ridge down the middle of it.
It looks like someone took a bite out of her nose
and it's the mark of two front teeth
with the gap in the middle.
She says when she was five
she walked into a car.

In a moment I am going to be wheeled
out of here on a bed,
they're going to put me to sleep
and bang my nose with a rubber hammer.

Poor Charlie.

Is It Possible to Sleep on a Train?

Can I sleep on the train?
Can I sleep on the train?
Can I sleep?

On the train
On the train
On the train
On the train
Can I sleep?

On the train
On the train
On the train
On the train
I sleep.

Great Day

Can't find the bathroom
Can't find my socks
Can't find the corn-flakes
Can't find the lunch-box
Can't find the book-folder
Can't find the front door
Can't find school
Can't find the class-room
Can't find the pen
Can't find the paper
Can't find the lunch-box
Can't find the pen
Can't find the paper
Can't find the way home
Can't find the front door
Can't find my plate
Can't find the television
Ah – find bed.

Eddie and the Supermarket

Shopping with Eddie was a nightmare.

I lift Eddie up and squeeze him into the seat
on the shopping trolley.
'In you get, little feller.'
So he goes rigid.
He turns himself into a little fat iron bar
that can't be bent.
I can't push his legs through the spaces.
'In you get, Eddie.'
Push.
'I said,
in
you
(push)
get
Eddie
(squeeze).'

Slowly he lets his legs relax
and I unbend them and thread them
into the trolley.

And off we go.
We're wheeling past the baked beans
and he leans out and grabs a can.
'Bince. More bince.'
'No, Eddie, we don't need any more beans.'
'Bince, bince, bince, bince, bince –'
'No, we don't need any beans.'

'Bince, bince, bince, bince, bince.'
'No beans, Eddie.'

We're heading now for the Kit Kats, Penguins, Topic bars
Crunchies, Milky Ways . . .
He stops shouting, 'Bince, bince bince . . .'
and he leans out of his seat
arms waving
we whizz round the corner of the
packs of chocolate wafers
and his chunky little hand grabs a packet.
'Wheeeeee – chocleet – wheeee.'

'We're going to take that packet back, Eddie.
We're going to take that packet back.'
Then there's an explosion:
'My chocleet. My chocleet. My chocleet.'

He turns into the little fat iron bar again.
In front of my eyes he becomes a screaming demon,
head flung back
face going red
eyes getting swollen
back stiff
hands punching out
body heaving to and fro.

A woman is looking at me
and saying to herself:
You're a torturer.
You're horrible to babies.

'My chocleet. Bince, bince, bince, bince.'

Some people walk about pretending
nothing is going on.
But I can tell they're in pain.
The noise of Eddie is getting into their bones.

People are moving away from us.
There's a man over there
hurrying to get to the kitchen rolls.
Eddie is wrenching the bars of the trolley,
'Chocleet bince. My chocleet bince.'
I want some kitchen rolls too.
So the man who's trying
to get away from me thinks
he's being hunted by Eddie.

Then one of the shelf-stackers
tries to be friendly.
He looks at the screaming blob called Eddie
and winks, does some useless trick with his finger
and says:
'Oooh it's not that bad, little one.'

Thank you, shelf-stacker, brilliant finger move.
'She is making a fuss, isn't she?'
says our jolly shelf-stacker.
Eddie is veering about so much
the shelf-stacker can't even tell it's a boy.
'Bince, bince, bince. Chocleet, chocleet, chocleet.'

I want to yell my head off too.
I want to run round the supermarket
waving my arms about
screaming, 'Bince, bince, bince.'
I want to sit in someone's trolley
and bend the bars
and drop baked bean cans on the floor
and grab chocolate biscuits
and drive my dad crazy.

Then the Security Men arrive.
They've come to collect the money
from the cash registers.
There's four of them.
They're huge –
in big padded blue uniforms
with crash helmets on
and truncheons in their belts.
This is my chance:
'Eddie, look who's come to get you!'

He looks
he looks
and he stops howling.

All round me people relax
they smile
they chat.
I glide through paying my bill.
We all float out into the car park.
Everything feels nice and easy.

When we get home
I find that I have forgotten to get
bread, jam, toilet rolls, milk
orange juice, tuna fish and corn-flakes.
'Dinner time, Eddie,' I say.
'What do you want?'
'Bince,' says Eddie.
I go to the cupboard.
He was right.
We have run out of beans.
I say:
'Eddie, I'm sorry but we've run out of beans.
No beans.'
And he says:
'Bince, bince, bince, bince, bince, bince . . .'

Miss Stafford

Miss Stafford marches across the floor
with her box of coloured chalks
to tell us the Bible stories.
There's Pharaoh's dreams
and only Joseph can say what they mean.
There's Abraham holding a knife
to the neck of his beloved son.
There are the nasty brothers
who throw Joseph down a well
because they're jealous of his
many-coloured coat.

Miss Stafford marches across the floor
with her box of coloured chalks
and she draws prisons and daggers
and mountains and city walls
but best of all
she draws Joseph's many-coloured coat:
green, red, blue, purple, yellow and white.
What a coat.
Every chalk in the box.
No wonder the brothers are jealous.

Miss Stafford marches across the floor
with her box of coloured chalks.

 * Rules *

Last one to the door is a smelly.

She's not allowed in my room

    when I've got my pants off.

First one to the door is a smelly.

He's not allowed to jump on my head

    before I wake up in the morning.

Second one to the door is a smelly.

He can't do a poo in here

    when I'm in the bath.

Anyone who gets to the door

is a smelly.

The Nest

Miss Goodall had this idea of having a Nature Table
and we all had to bring into school
things we'd found.

Soon the table was piled high with stuff:
brambles, acorns, worms, woodlice
dead leaves . . .

So Miss Goodall said,
'No need to bring in any more Nature things
thank you very much.
What we're going to do now
is have a Wall Chart. A Nature Watch.
I want you to write up on the chart
the date, your name
and What You Have Observed.'

It started off OK.
11/10/54, Sheena Maclean, I saw a robin.
12/10/54, Melanie Baxter, Today there was a duck.
But it wasn't long before
it started turning into a competition.
14/10/54, Michael Rosen, I saw a robin *and* a duck.

Things were getting
pretty hot
round the Nature Chart.

One night
while I was walking home
through the Memorial Park
I was getting to thinking about
what I could write up tomorrow
on the Nature Chart.
Wouldn't it be great
to see something really good
on the way home from school?
Like a
walrus.
Then I thought about how it would be great
to find a nest of baby animals.
Like a nest of baby vultures.
I remembered how
I had once seen a film
of a bird that lays its eggs on the ground.
Well –
I could find a nest on the ground,
couldn't I?
Trouble was
there were no nests on the ground
in the Memorial Park.
But there *was* plenty of dead grass lying around . . .
. . . so maybe I could pick up some of this dead grass
and make something.

I twisted the grass around
poked it about
and I made something
that looked like a bird's nest.

27

Then I worked out a plan
that would *prove* it was a nest.
When I got to school the next day
everyone would think I was brilliant
at Nature.

I left my nest lying on the ground
and walked home.
Next morning, my friend Harrybo calls for me
and off we go to school
through the Memorial Park.

So I say to Harrybo:
'Hey, let's walk over this way, eh?'
'No,' he says.
'Go on,' I say, 'we might find *something*.'
'Oh, O K,' he says.
So I led off in the direction of the nest.

funny
sort of
nest

I didn't want to lead him there
and find it.
He might get suspicious
and say it was a trick.
I wanted us to see it together,
maybe him a little bit first
then he'd believe it was real.
Good plan . . . the only trouble was:
I couldn't see it anywhere.
I didn't know where to lead him.
Maybe it had blown away.
'Come on,' says Harrybo, 'or we'll be late.'
'No, hang on,' I say.
'What are you doing?' he says.
'Oh, you know. Just looking for Nature,
come on over here. You look.'

Then I saw it.
The nest.
It was still there.
He wasn't going to see it.
My plan wasn't working.
So I just pretended not to look surprised
and said:
'Hey Harrybo, I don't suppose this is anything, is it?'
He comes over.
'Michael. That's a nest.
That
is
a
nest.'
'Is it?' I say.
'Yep. Amazing. That's what it is all right.
That's a nest.
We could take that into school,' he says,
'and write it up on the Nature Chart.
No one's ever found a nest before.
Incredible.'

So we picked up the nest
and took it into school.
We put it on Miss Goodall's table
and all the other kids crowded round:
'Where did you find it?'
'It's brilliant.'
'It could be an eagle's.'

Harrybo put on his important voice
and said,
'Look, er, don't touch it, O K?
It's a bird's nest.
We were looking for Nature
and we spotted it.
I knew it was a nest straight away.'

Miss Goodall looked at us
and looked at the nest.
She had a way of raising one eyebrow
and smiling
if she thought something funny was going on.
'Looks to me,' she said, 'like someone made it.
Some little fingers or other made it.'

I looked at it sitting on her table.
It didn't look much like a bird's nest at all.
In fact, it looked just like what it was:
a heap of dead grass that someone had twisted about a bit.

But Harrybo was quite cross:
'Oh no Miss Goodall,' he says.
'We found this when we were looking for Nature.
It was there on the ground.
Actually Miss,
if Michael hadn't said
let's go over the grassy bit
we'd've missed it.
That was really lucky he said that.'

Miss Goodall now looked at *me* very hard.
Her eyebrow still up.
I said nothing.
'Can we write it up on the Nature Chart, now?'
says Harrybo.
'Not just now,' says Miss Goodall,
'it's assembly time.'

Now we didn't get to writing it up
all that day.
Or the next.
The nest sat on her table
getting looser and looser
until all it was
was a heap of dead grass.

I hated looking at it.
Surely everyone could see now
it was all a big trick.
Someone was bound to say
that we made it.
Then I would go red
and I would be shown up
in front of everybody.
But no one said anything.
And Harrybo
kept going on about
what a Great Find it was.
I started to wish he'd just shut up about it,
or someone would steal it.

A week or two later
we got to school one day
and the nest was gone.
So was the Nature Chart.
Harrybo said,
'Miss Goodall,
why have you taken down the Nature Chart?'
'Oh,' she said,
'I thought it was time for a change.
Anyway,' she says, looking at me,
'things were getting a bit
silly
don't you think?'
'Were they?' I said.
'Yes,' she said,
'they were.
But if you want your nest back, boys
I've put it under the sink.'
'That's OK,' I said.
'I haven't really got anywhere to put it.'
'I have,' said Harrybo, 'brilliant.
I'll take it home, Miss, and keep it in my room.
When you come over my place, Michael
you can look at it any time you like.'
'Thanks.'

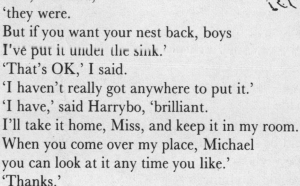

That night he took it home
put it on his chest of drawers
and every time I go over to his place
he shows it to me.
He never lets me forget the great day
we found a real bird's nest
on the ground
at Memorial Park.
He never seems to wonder
why I don't jump up and down
and get as excited as he does.
He just loves looking at it,
thinking about the bird that made it.

The Torch

I nagged my mum and dad for a torch.
'Oh go on. I'd love a torch.
One of those ones with black rubber round them.
Go on. Pleeeeeeese.'
It was no good. I wasn't getting anywhere.

Then came my birthday.
On the table was a big box
in the box
a torch.
My dad took it out the box.
'You see that torch,' he says
'It's waterproof.
That is a waterproof torch.'

Waterproof. Wow!

So that night I got into the bath
and went underwater swimming with it.
Breathe in,
under the water,
switch on
search for shipwrecks
and treasure.
Up, breathe
under again
exploring the ocean floor.

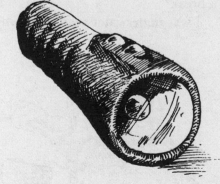

Then the torch went out.

I shook it and banged it but it wouldn't go.
I couldn't get it to go again.
My birthday torch.
So I got out, dried myself off
put on my pyjamas and went into the kitchen.

'The – er – torch won't work. It's broken.'
And my dad says,
'What do you mean, "it's broken"?
It couldn't have just broken.
How did it break?'
'I dunno, it just went off.'

'I don't believe it. You ask him a simple question
and you never get a simple answer.
You must have been
doing something with it.'
'No. It just went off.'
'Just try telling the truth, will you?
How
did
it
break?'
'I was underwater swimming with it.'

'Are you mad?
When I said the torch is waterproof
I meant it keeps the rain off.
I didn't mean you could go deep-sea diving with it.
Ruined. Completely ruined.
For weeks and weeks he nags us stupid that he wants
one of these waterproof torches
and then first thing he does is wreck it.
How long did it last?
Two minutes? Three minutes?
These things cost money, you know.
Money.'

I felt so rotten.
My birthday torch.

At the weekend, he says,
We're going into Harrow to take the torch back.

We walk into the shop,
my dad goes up to the man at the counter
and says:
'You see this torch.
I bought it from you a couple of weeks ago
It's broken.'

So the man picks it up.
'It couldn't have just broken,' says the man,
'how did it break?'
And my dad says,
'I dunno, it just went off.'
'Surely you must have been doing something
with it.'
'No, no, no,' says my dad,
'it just went off.'
'Come on,' says the man, 'these torches don't just break
down.'
So I said
'Well, actually, I was in the –'
and I got a hard kick on the ankle from my dad.
'I was in the, you know, er kitchen and it went off.'

So the man said that he would take it out the back
to show Len.
He came back a few minutes later and said that Len
couldn't get it to work either
so he would send it back to the makers.
'You'll have to have a new one,' he says.
'I should think so too,' says my dad.
'Thank YOU.'

Outside the shop
my dad says to me,
'What's the matter with you?
Are you crazy?
You were going to tell him all about your underwater
swimming fandango, weren't you?
Blabbermouth!'

Robin Hood's Bay

It was summertime
and it was hot.
We were on holiday in Yorkshire.
My friend Paul said:
'Why don't we go and explore the old railway tunnel?'
and I said:
'Yeah, good idea.'

So we did.
We left our mums and dads at the tents.
When we got there
the tunnel was dark
all the bricks were covered in black soot
from the smoke of the old steam engines
that used to run through.
You couldn't see the other end.
It was like a great, empty, black space in front of us.

Paul said:
'I don't think I want to go in there.'
and I said:
'What shall we do then?'
and he said:
'We could walk to the station.'
and I said:
'Yeah, good idea.'

So we did.
We walked along the old railway tracks
to the station.
As we walked
we jumped from sleeper to sleeper
and did horrible things to slugs.

When we got to the station, Paul said:
'How much money have you got?'
and I said:
'Two and six.' (That's about 13p nowadays)
and he said:
'Me too. We could go to Robin Hood's Bay
and back with that.'
and I said:
'Yeah, good idea.'

So we did.
On the train
by the sea
through the sand dunes
over bridges
along the cliff tops.

When we got to Robin Hood's Bay
we walked along the beach
we paddled in the sea
we diddled along in the wet sand
and Paul said:
'There are fossils here, you know.'
and I said:
'Are there?'
and he said:
'Let's look for some.'
and I said:
'Yeah, good idea.'

So we did.
We picked up hundreds and hundreds of stones.
They were a sort of grey-blue colour.
We didn't find any fossils.
There was a stream though
and we piled up stones in the river
to make a dam.
Hundreds and hundreds of stones.
It didn't dam the river
it made a kind of bridge.

Then Paul said:
'I think we ought to go back soon.'
and I said:
'Yeah, good idea.'

So we did.
We caught the train back:
by the sea
through the sand dunes
over bridges
along the cliff tops.
We walked back along the tracks
to the tents.

Just as we were nearly there
I saw Paul's dad.
He had a pair of binoculars in his hand:
they were muddy.
He started shouting:
'Here they are! Here they are!
Here they are!'
and he was waving his arms.
He rushed up to us.
'Where have you been?
Where have you been?'
and Paul said:
'Robin Hood's Bay. It was really good.'
and Paul's dad said:
'Robin Hood's Bay? Robin Hood's Bay?'

Just then, I saw my mum and dad.
They were running up the road
and shouting to Paul's dad:
'Where did you find them?'
Paul's dad looked up at the sky
shook his head and
raised his arms and he said:
'They've been to Robin Hood's Bay,
would you believe!'
and my dad said:
'Robin Hood's Bay? Robin Hood's Bay?
They must be out of their minds.'
and Paul's dad said:
'We've been hunting for you, for hours.
We've been worried sick.
We thought you were stuck in the tunnel.
I thought you may have been run down
by a train.
We've been all over the cliffs looking for you.
We thought you might have fallen down the cliffs.'

My dad said:
'Why did you go to Robin Hood's Bay?
Whose idea was that?'
and Paul said:
'It was my idea. All my own idea.'
and my dad and Paul's dad looked at me and said:
'Paul's idea? Paul's idea?
What did *you* say to Paul
when he came up with this idea?'
And I said:
'I thought it was a good idea.'
and they said:
'A good idea? A good idea?
for goodness' sake, You're older than him.
He's only seven. You're ten years old.
You know better than that.
We've got to go and phone the police now.'
and Paul said:
'Can I come?'
and Paul's dad said:
'No you can't.
I've got to go and tell them
that we've found you
and they don't have to get the helicopter out
looking for you.'
and Paul said:
'OK Dad.'
I just stood there.

After that we went off to have something to eat.
It wasn't lunch
because it was after lunch-time.
It wasn't tea
because it was after tea-time.

Paul's dad didn't speak to me for the rest of the holiday.
Actually he's scarcely spoken to me ever since.

The Line

When the new school was opened we had to line up, Girl here, Boy there, Girl here, Boy there. Miss Wheelock, who was the Headmaster's Deputy Sheriff, said: 'In this school, there will be a Boys' Playground and a Girls' Playground. I want you all to draw an imaginary line between the top of the steps *here*, over to the edge of the United Dairies on the other side of the fence up *there*. I don't ever want to see any boy crossing the Line in morning playtime, dinner-time, or afternoon playtime and I don't want to see anyone loitering *along* the Line.'

In the first week I was at the new school, I got to know a girl called Frances who tried to teach me how to skip. This was difficult because she had to stand on one side of the Imaginary Line and I had to stand on the other. First of all she skipped for a bit and then, carefully making sure her feet kept to her side, she passed the skipping rope over the Line to me – where I was making sure my feet were keeping to my side. Then I skipped.

Miss Wheelock saw this and said, 'I'm going to put a stop to this. If you want to learn how to skip, boy, then bring your own skipping rope. I've said: I don't want anyone crossing the Line. Passing a skipping rope *over* the Line is just the same as *crossing* the Line, isn't it? Frances, I'm surprised at you. I thought you knew better.'

I thought: that's funny. We've only been at the new school a week. Why's she surprised at Frances but she wasn't surprised at me? Not long after this, something much more serious happened to us and the Line.

Gunter the German brought a ball to school that said 'Handball' on it. Someone kicked it and we all went haring across the Line to get it. The whistle went off and Miss Wheelock screamed. She wanted everyone to stop moving. 'Everyone stop moving. Stop moving. Stop moving. I want that ball Gunter,' she said, 'I want that ball.'

Gunter didn't know what was going on except he wasn't going to give the ball to anyone – least of all to her. 'I want that ball, Gunter,' she said, 'and by God, I'll have it, boy.' So she started off walking across the playground towards him.

There was the playground, absolutely still, with all of us standing there, like skittles all over it, except for Miss Wheelock marching for Gunter the German's Handball. All boys one side of the Imaginary Line. All girls on the other. Except for a group of us, miles *over* the Line. It took ages for her to get to us.

'Give me that ball, Gunter,' she said, 'I want it.' Gunter didn't say anything. He just held on to it a bit harder, hugging it to his chest. He couldn't speak English. He'd only been in England a week or two and he was still wearing his yellow shoes.

Miss Wheelock prodded the Handball. 'Ball – Gunter – Ball.' Gunter hugged the Handball. Everyone else for miles and miles, right the way across the playground was standing still, right up as far as the climbing frame in the Nursery playground. No one talked.

So Miss Wheelock got her hands round the German's Handball and heaved on it. But he wouldn't let go. It was *his* Handball. Miss Wheelock and him were still heaving on it and she was still screaming. 'Ball – Gunter – ball,' when I booed.

And the moment *I* booed, Harrybo booed and all of us
who had run all this way over the Line booed.
But Miss Wheelock, who was bigger than
Gunter, even though she was a tiny grown-up,
actually got hold of the Handball and
wrenched it out of Gunter's hands.

Gunter started gulping in big sobs but he didn't say
anything. She turned on us and said, 'Never,
never, never, in all my time –' when suddenly
up the steps at the end of the Imaginary Line,
came the Headmaster.

We stopped booing. The whole thing had got too big for
booing. But he had seen what was going on.
'You,' he says, 'You – you – you – and you.'
And, no trouble, he knew which ones of us to
get, because we were standing there, the only
boys out of the whole school, in girl-country.

'You – you – you,' he said, 'go straight to my study and *no*
running.' Then he turned to Miss Wheelock,
his Deputy Sheriff and said, 'Are you *all right*,
Miss Wheelock?' And Miss Wheelock took out
her hankie and dried the corners of her mouth.

It was miles and miles to his room and all the way I was
thinking: I started the booing, so I'll be the
one to get it. On the way there, there were
hundreds of girls' faces right down to the
tinies, all watching. Though some of them
were so good they didn't even dare look at us.
They just stared at the ground afraid if they
looked into our eyes, they'd catch some of our
evil spirit.

Gunter was still gulping. He didn't know what was going
on. He hadn't done anything wrong. Miss
Wheelock had. She had stolen his Handball.
'Come in. Come in,' said the Headmaster,
breathing through his nose and quivering his
nostrils. *I'll make them hear me breathing. I'll make
them hear every bit of breath I've got. Up* and *down
my nose. They'll learn what it means to break my
rules and boo my teachers.*

'Why do we have the Line? Eh? What's it for? For fun?
For my amusement? You! Why do we have the
Line?' No one knew why we had the Line.
'Come on. Come on. Come on. Don't waste
any more of my time.' 'Because they're girls
sir.' It wasn't what he wanted.

'You! Why do we have the Line?' 'I don't know, sir.'
'You!' 'I don't know, sir.' 'You!' 'I don't know,
sir.' 'Then I'll tell you why.' He was walking
about all over the place.

51

'Because I knew, long before we moved into these
buildings that your parents have paid for, that
there would be trouble from children like you.
And I sat down here in this room and I
thought: How am I going to stop that little
group of boys – and it will be boys – and there
are always some in every school – how am I
going to stop them from spoiling everything for
everyone else?

'"Well," I said to myself, "maybe it does seem as if it
always happens like that but it's not going to
happen in *my* school."' And it was Miss
Wheelock who put me on to it: "The trouble,"
she said, "always starts in the playground.
That's where the trouble starts." And I think
she's right.

'I come out on to the playground. And there you are. *That
little group*. Screaming about amongst the girls,
spoiling their games, then daring to catcall
Miss Wheelock: the school's Deputy Head
Teacher. You must think we're mad to even –'
'At my last school, sir, we –' 'But you're at *this*
school, boy.'

So he gave us the cane three times for going into girl-
country and three times for booing. He did the
caning with a bamboo stick, bringing it down
on our hands as fast and as hard as he could.
'I'm putting this down in a book,' he said,
'where it will never be forgotten.'

Talking-tubes

I believe everything my brother tells me
that's why I know about talking-tubes in old houses.

Once we went to this old house
and the guide who was taking us round
told us that there were tubes
running through the massive great thick walls
so that the people in the olden days
could talk to each other.

After the guide went off
my brother explained to me
that these talking-tubes were only discovered
a short while ago.
He said they were closed up
with great big corks.

We are not
amused!

He said,
when the people who discovered them
pulled the corks out
they heard
all these old words from hundreds of years ago.
They heard knights-in-armour talking.
What they said just came tumbling out of the talking-tubes.
Amazing.

I believe everything my brother tells me
that's why I know about talking-tubes in old houses.

Trousers Down

My best friend Mart said that
we could take rucksacks and drinks
and sandwiches and raisins and chocolate and
go and climb The Sugarloaf.

I said that it was miles and we might get lost
but he said he knew how to read maps
and we had walked 15 miles in a day before
when we went with our parents.

So we did,
we climbed The Sugarloaf
all on our own
with our rucksacks.

It's a mountain with one bit in Wales
and one bit in England.
We were so pleased when we got to the top
we said we ought to celebrate.
We discussed this as we sat at the top
eating our sandwiches and raisins and chocolate.

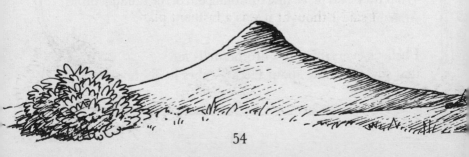

'I know,' said Mart,
'I've got it.
You see that path down there?
That's the way we go to get home.
Somewhere along that path
is the border between Wales and England.
We leave Wales and we go into England.
What we do,' he said,
'is we celebrate by walking into England
with our trousers down.'

'But how will we know where the border is?'
I said.
'Well,' he said,
'I don't know exactly where it is
but by looking at the map
I've got a pretty good idea.
So when I say we're getting near
to the border
we take our trousers down.
Then for the next few minutes
we walk along with our trousers down
until I reckon from the map
that we're in England.
What do you think?'

I said I thought it was a brilliant plan.

So we packed up our stuff
and headed down the mountain.
Mart was studying the map
and then he suddenly said,
'We're getting there.
Trousers down!'

So we took our trousers down
and our underpants
and we started walking on down the path.
It wasn't very easy because you can't take
very big strides with trousers and pants
round your ankles
but we kept on.

I said,
'What if we see someone, Mart?'
'We'll have to pull our trousers up
and wait till they're gone,' he says,
'then we take our trousers down again
and carry on.
We can't give up just because some people
turn up.'
'That's true,' I said.

So we walked on and Mart started singing
'We're walking into England with our trousers down
with our trousers down
with our trousers down.
We're walking into England with our trousers down
oh yeah!'

Nobody did turn up
and after quite some time
I said,
'Are we in England yet, Mart?'
And he studied the map and said,
'Yeah we must be by now.'
So we pulled our pants and trousers up
and headed back to the campsite.

When we got back
our mums and dads asked us how we got on:
'Did you climb right to the top of The Sugarloaf?'
'Oh yes,' said Mart, 'no problem.'
'But you must have walked something like fifteen miles,'
my dad said.
'That's it,' said Mart.
'Well done, boys,' said Mart's dad.
And I was feeling really proud so I said,
'And we walked into England with our trousers down.'

There was silence.
'You what?' said my dad.
'We walked into England with our trousers down.'
'Why in heaven's name did you do that?' he said.
'To celebrate. We had climbed The Sugarloaf.'

'Do you understand that, Connie?'
my dad said to my mum,
'Do you?'
He turned to Mart's parents:
'What have we done?
We've brought up two completely crazy children.
They go out, they climb a mountain,
they walk fifteen miles,
they read maps
they carry their own food and drink
they show themselves to be really capable,
responsible boys
and then what do they do?
They walk all over the countryside
with their trousers down.
How come we've produced two complete idiots.
Where did we go wrong?'

I thought,
wrong? wrong?
You haven't gone wrong.
Me and Mart
did something really brilliant today.
I mean,
I bet there's not many people in the world
who can say that they've walked into England
with their trousers down.

Motto

The motto on the wall said,
'Seek and ye shall find'.
I looked for it everywhere
but it was stuck to my behind.

The Register

Right Class 6
register time –
that means everyone sitting down.
Everyone, Darren.
No, Darren, we're not feeding the snails now.
Sarah, could you pass me the register?
No I haven't got it, you've got it.
You went to fetch it, remember?
Oh that was yesterday was it?
Darren, leave the snails alone.
One moment everyone, Mr Hardware wants a word.
Right Class 6
Mr Hardware says that any tennis balls landing
in the gutter by the kitchen will be left there till
Christmas
when they'll be sent to Dr Barnardo's.
No, he's not my doctor, Louise
my doctor doesn't need tennis balls
Dr Barnardo's not alive he's –
I know, Wayne, that if he's not alive
he can't use the tennis balls.
Darren, don't touch the snails, do you hear me?
Does anyone know who or what is Dr Barnardo's?
No Hugh, not a dog's home.
Yes Abdul, a children's home, well done.
I wonder Mrs Morris –
I don't want to be rude –
but I'm just settling the children down,

perhaps you could see a way to leaving now,
mmm?

I'm sure David is OK, Mrs Morris.

Yes, cake-making on Friday will be lovely, Mrs Morris
but –

Wayne that is very rude.

We've talked about kissing before.

If Mrs Morris wants to kiss David goodbye
that's OK and you've no right to laugh at –

thank you again Mrs Morris, yes biscuit-making too
that'll be lovely, thank you so much,

goodbye Mrs Morris,

she's not waving to you, Sophie.

Yes Colin?

Well, I'm sure Mr Hardware means any kind of ball
footballs, basketballs.

You got a baseball from your American cousin.

That was very nice of him.

No I don't know who won the World Series.

I can't guess because I don't know the names
of any of the baseball teams.

Ah – Mrs Riley, good morning,

Right Class 6

Mrs Riley says that if anyone who usually has school
dinner

on a Thursday but wants a school packed lunch for the
outing

to the Science Museum, then could they fill in the form.

Yes Judy?

The form.

Well, I'm not quite sure what form for the moment
but I'm sure a form will be coming along soon.
They usually do.
And I'll tell you when it does.
Well, if you don't want a school packed lunch
and you don't bring a packed lunch
then you'll be very hungry, won't you?
Darren, I don't want to have to tell you about the snails
again
we're doing the register now, not snails,
Yes, Zoë I know quite well that I'm not actually doing the
register
at this very second
but I will be
and I would be
and I could be . . .
Do you know what the time is, Mervyn?
You do.
Do you know how many minutes late you are, Mervyn?
You do.
Do you know why you're late every morning, Mervyn?
You do.
Do you have any idea how we are going to get you
to come to school on time, Mervyn?
You don't.
Mark and Hong are sitting very nicely.
Ah Mrs Morris, you're back.
Yes, we could make toffee as well
an excellent idea . . .
Qui-et!

There'll be no toffee for anyone
if there's that kind of noise . . .
thank you so much Mrs Morris
I'm sure we have the right pans for making toffee
but I can't look just now
bye bye yes of course, bye bye.
Rasheda, Jason, Simone all sitting very nicely
Darren not sitting nicely.
Not sitting at all in fact.
Oh no he's left the lid off,
quick, Abdul
the lid
put the lid back on the snails.
What? One's missing.
Which one?
No not all of you.
Everyone come back,
sit down.
Abdul and just Abdul
can you tell us which snail is missing?
Robin.
Was Robin in the aquarium before?
Darren?
No Mervyn, snails don't eat each other.
You know they eat leaves.
All term we've been looking at how they eat leaves
we've written poems about how they eat leaves
we've drawn graphs of how many leaves they eat in a day
and now you're telling me that they eat each other.
You know sometimes I wonder why we've got these snails
here.

It really isn't anything to cry about Paul.
I know Robin was your favourite
and I'm sure Batman doesn't miss him.
I'm not sure snails do miss each other.
Look, I don't want to deal with this just now.
I'm sure Robin will turn up,
he can't have gone far.
Snails don't gallop do they?
Darren, is that the truth?
Is what Salima is saying true?
Is it?
Well, take Robin out of your pocket right now,
put him back in the aquarium
and go straight downstairs to see Mrs Rashid
and you can explain to her what you did to Robin.
I'm not sure you'll be here for Mrs Morris's baking day
at this rate.
Ah who's this?
John.
No, I'm sorry John you can't have the register
just yet.
Tell Mrs Riley we'll be down with it in just a moment.
Right Class 6.
The register.
Oh – where is it?
It was here just a moment ago.
Can anyone see the register?
Can anyone see the register?

The Wedding

Uncle Ronnie got married in *shul**,
my dad was the best man,
there they all were standing under the *khuppe***,
and the Rabbi is talking,
and *Bubbe**** is watching from her wheelchair,
and it's time for my dad to hand Ronnie the ring.

Out it comes and just as my dad gives it to him,
Ronnie faints.
Out cold.
Bubbe starts crying
and everyone in the *shul* starts talking and tutting.
So the bride's brother got his shoulder in tight on Ronnie
on one side
and my dad got his shoulder in tight on Ronnie
on the other
and the *shammes***** propped him up from behind
and that was how Uncle Ronnie got married.

Bubbe said later it was a terrible shame
he missed it.

*shul = synagogue
**khuppe = canopy for wedding ceremonies
***Bubbe = grandmother
****shammes = synagogue helper

Gypsy

My mother looks in the mirror
and says, there's gypsy in me.
She pulls a red scarf
tight over her head
and ties it at the back of her neck.
How can she be a gypsy? we say to each other.

When Uncle Ronnie got married
an old woman who I'd never seen before
sat next to *Bubbe**.
She had gold earrings and a gold tooth
her skin was dark
she laughed at the food
and pointed at me saying:
who's this? somebody tell me who this young man is?

Who was she? I asked later.
Bubbe's sister, they told me.
I never saw her again
She was wearing a scarf
tight over her head
tied at the back.

*Bubbe = grandmother

Muss i'den

Our giggly German teacher, Miss Joseph, said:
'This year I want to teach you a little Austrian folk song
hee hee hee . . .'

And she began singing:
'*Muss i'den, muss i'* –'

There was a sudden rush of air on the back row
and Pat Phipps screamed:
'YAAAAAAAAAAAAA!'
Miss Joseph was appalled:
'Pat, really! How unlike you. What is going on?'
'Miss, it's Elvis,' said Pat.

Miss Joseph had been teaching *Muss i'den*
to her German classes for 20 years.

She didn't know that Elvis Presley, the King,
the greatest rock singer ever
the man who was God to Pat Phipps
and very nearly every other girl in the world
was at that very moment stationed in Germany.

68

She didn't know that Elvis Presley, the King,
the greatest rock singer ever
the man who was God to Pat Phipps
and very nearly every other girl in the world
had that week,
given the world the song 'Wooden Heart'.
A song, that had the chorus and the tune of
Miss Joseph's little Austrian folk song:
Muss i'den.

That's why Pat Phipps screamed:
'YAAAAAAAAAAAAA!'

Pat Phipps explained all this to Miss Joseph.
Miss Joseph was still appalled.
Pat Phipps was still trembling.
So Miss Joseph said,
'Well, class, perhaps we won't do
Muss i'den this year.
Open your books at page 71 . . .'

The Shop Downstairs

We live in a flat over a shop.
It's an estate agent's called Norman and Butt.
My father told me that Norman is the talkative one.
'He's full of big ideas. He rushes in
and starts gabbling away with what they're going to do,
things like:
"We could open a new shop,
we could buy new desks
we could be millionaires"
and then Mr Butt says:
"But –"
and so nothing happens.
That's them, Norman and Butt,'
says my dad.
'Is that true?' we say.
'Sure it is.'

Berwick-on-Tweed

The sign in the window said,

Top Board

After three weeks of swimming lessons
Mr Hicks the swimming teacher said,
'OK Michael, I want you to dive off the top board.'

WHAT?!
Is he crazy? I can't do that.
The board is miles up in the air.
When people dive off there
they drop through the air
at a hundred miles an hour.

I've only ever dived off the side before.
Just lean forward and flop.

'Up you go lad, just pretend it's the side
and just go, lad, go,' says Mr Hicks.

Up I go
I stand on the board . . .

. . . the big clock at the other end of the pool
is just the same height as me.
The paint is peeling off the ceiling.
It's hotter up here
and the air is full of shouting.
Underneath my feet it feels like sandpaper . . .

'. . . Just pretend it's the side
and just go, lad, go . . .'

So I did.
It felt like doing a handstand on nothing.
It felt like my belly was going into my legs.
When I hit the water
it was like someone walloping me in the face.

'Well, done,' said Mr Hicks.
'I want five more of those before the end of the lesson.'

Butter or Margarine

Row, row, row your boat,
gently down the stream;
merrily, merrily, merrily, merrily,
life is but a –

no it's not, it's margarine.

Stobs

My best friend at the new school is Stobs.
We got together because I sat at the back of the class
making faces.
He already had a best friend, Staff
but all three of us get on really well.

Me and Stobs had this idea of making a book about
London
We'd collect postcards and take pictures, we said, yeah.
And we'd go places like reporters and say what we'd seen,
yeah.
You know, like under Charing Cross Bridge and interview
tramps.
Or we could go to posh places like Harrods or the Ritz
and write down what they said when they chucked us out,
yeah.

We went out and bought a scrap-book
and stuck in it a postcard of Westminster Abbey
and Stobs drew a picture of the coat of arms of London.
He said I could do the writing and he could do the
pictures
because he was really good at drawing, yeah
and we could go to Hampstead Heath,
like we were on safari and report back from there.

Next day at school, I was telling Staff about how me and
Stobs
were making a London scrap-book thing.
Later that day Stobs came up to me
his face all glowering and furious.
'You told Staff about the London thing, didn't you?'
'Yep,' I said.
'Right, that's it,' he said. 'Right.'
And he walked off.

I thought, what's going on? I haven't done anything
wrong.
All I did was tell Staff about the London thing.

I ran after him.
'Look Stobs, all . . .'
He cut me dead.
He just looked straight through me.
He didn't want to talk to me.
I remembered feeling kind of desperate.
All tight round my chest.
I mean
he was the person I'd decided to be my friend
at the new school
and now he was like an enemy.

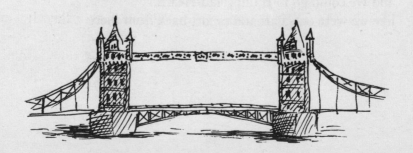

I tried talking to him
I tried saying sorry.
I tried saying, what was wrong with telling Staff?
All I got was this fat sulky look.
He just ignored me.
I hated him for making me feel so bad.

Staff quickly sussed that something was wrong
and he grabbed me and said,
'What's going on, what's all this about?'
'Nothing,' I said, 'no, no, no, nothing.'
I was too embarrassed to say.
I thought the whole thing had got too daft to talk about.
'Come on,' he says, 'tell me, is it to do with Stobs?'
'Yes, he's not talking to me.'
'Why not?'
'I don't want to say,' I said.
'Just tell me,' says Staff.
'He's really angry I told you about the London thing.'
'And he's not talking to you just for that?' he says.
'Yep.'
'Oh that's rubbish,' says Staff, 'he's always like that.'
'You mean he's done that sort of thing to you?'
'Oh yeah,' he says, 'loads of times.'

That got me thinking.
I had thought it was all to do with *me*.
That there was something *I* had done wrong.
That it was bad of me to have told Staff about the London
thing.
Now I realized it was all in Stobs.
All it was, was something that Stobs did to his friends.

From that moment on
I didn't try to talk to him.
I didn't even give him the chance to ignore me
and cut me dead.
I went off and knocked around with some of the other
guys,
Rodge and Nell.

A day later
I'm packing my bag at the back of the class
and Stobs is there and he says,
'Don't forget your maths book,
he wants the work in tomorrow.'

GREETINGS FROM LONDON

Don't Tell Your Mother

When my mum goes to evening classes
my dad says,
'Don't tell your mother – let's have *matzo bray**.
She always says:
"Don't give the boys that greasy stuff.
It's bad for them."
So don't tell her, all right?'

So he breaks up the *matzos*
puts them into water to soften them up.
Then he fries them
till they're glazed and crisp.

'It tastes best like this,
fried in *hinner shmaltz***,
skimmed off the top of the chicken soup,'
he says,
'but olive oil will do.'

Then he beats up three eggs
and pours it on over the frying *matzos*
till it's all cooked.

It tastes brilliant.
We love it.
Then we wash everything up
absolutely everything
and we go to bed.

Next day,
Mum says to us,
'What did your father cook you last night?'

Silence.

'What did your father cook you last night?'

'Oh you know . . . stuff . . .
. . . egg on toast, I think.'

* *matzo bray* = the Yiddish name of a dish made of
matzos and egg. *Matzo* is the word for unleavened
bread that tastes like water biscuits.
** *hinner shmaltz* = the Yiddish words for chicken fat

Leosia

I went to see my father's cousin Michael.
He was born in Poland.

When the Nazis came in the west
his parents put him on a train
going east
and he never saw them again.
They died in a Nazi death camp.

When the Russians came in the east
he was arrested, put on a train
and sent to one of the Russian camps.
But he lived.

When I went to see him
he wouldn't tell me any of this.
When he went out of the room
his wife said he can't bear to talk about it.
When he came back into the room
he said, 'Tell him the story about my cousin Leosia.'

So they told me the story about cousin Leosia.

'When the Nazis came in the west
Leosia pretended to be a Christian.
She put a crucifix round her neck
and then she fetched her grandmother's brooch
and took the diamonds off it.
She took the soles off the heels of her shoes
put the diamonds inside the heels
and put the soles back on.
She thought if there were going to be any problems
she would be able to sell them.
Then she went west
into Germany.

In Germany she worked in a factory.
No one ever found out that she was Jewish.

At the end of the war
she couldn't face going back to Poland.
Her parents, all her friends and all her relations
had been taken away to the camps and killed.

She went to Israel to find her brother Naftali.

She told him how she had lived
right through the war
with diamonds in the heels of her shoes.
'I always knew if ever I got into difficulty
I could've sold them
and maybe paid someone to help me.
And here they are,' she said,
'the very diamonds themselves.'

And Naftali said, 'Where did you get the diamonds from,
Leosia?'
And Leosia said, 'From our grandmother's brooch.'

So Naftali said, 'Listen carefully, Leosia.
Many years ago, our grandmother wrote to me.
She said that grandfather's business wasn't doing too well
and so to help out,
she had taken the diamonds off her brooch
put in glass ones instead
and sold off the diamonds.
She didn't tell anyone about it
but she wrote to me to get it off her chest.
You went through the whole war
with nothing more than
bits of glass in the heels of your shoes.'

Australia

We went to Australia.
It was a great time for beasties.
They were all over us:
ants, mosquitoes, spiders, stick insects, lizards
horse flies . . .
even the birds in Australia fly out of the sky at you.
You walk under a tree where a magpie's nesting
and it dive bombs you:
eeeeeeeeeooooooooowwwwwwww.
You have to duck out the way
or you end up with a magpie stuck in your head.

We went to stay in the bush.
(You know that doesn't mean we were staying in *a* bush.
like: 'Mm, it's really prickly in here.'
No, the 'bush' means the countryside.)
We were staying in a little old house.
Next door to the house was the outside toilet
and next door to that was another little old house
where the children were going to sleep.
First night we were there I said,
'OK, off you go to the toilet,
then off to your little house
and I'll come and tuck you in in a moment.'
I sat down to read something
when I heard this screaming noise from outside:
'Yeeeeee.'
'Ahhhhhh'

'Oiiiiiiiiii'
I rushed out to see what was going on
and my kids were standing outside the toilet
screaming,
'THERE'S A SPIDER IN THE TOILET, DAD.'
I said,
'I don't believe it.
We've travelled all these thousands of miles
and first night we get there, all you can say is:
"There's a spider in the toilet, Dad."
'NO DAD, IT'S HORRIBLE
IT'S GOING TO EAT US WHILE WE'RE
DOING IT.'
'OK,' I said, 'I'll go in there and have a look.'
I looked.
Up, down, round, behind.
'Nope. No spider in there.'
'IT IS. IT'S UP THERE ON THE WALL.
IT'S GOING TO DROP ON US
WHILE WE'RE SITTING THERE.'
I said,
'I tell you there is no spider in there
at all –'
(I was looking all round)
'– no spider anywh–'
And there it was.
Up on the wall.
A great grey furry thing
all quivery
it's beady little eyes staring at me

like it was growling:
'*Grrrrrrrrrrrrrrrrrrrrr*'
I started backing off,
'Look kids, don't worry about it,
just go in there, do what you've got to do
and get out again.'
And they're pushing me back into the toilet.
'NO, GET RID OF IT, DAD.
IT'S GOING TO EAT USSSSSSSS.'
So I said,
'OK, OK. Course I'm not scared.
Sure I'll get rid of it.'
But as I got up to it,
I thought, how *do* you get rid of it?
Go up to it? and say?
'Hi.
We're just in from England.
I'm Mike. These are my children.
Can we use your toilet?'
But it went on looking at me:
'*Grrrrrrrrrrrrrrrrrrrrr*'
So I looked round for something to get it with.
And I found it:
the toilet brush.
Perfect.
I know what I'll do:
There's a gap between the top of the wall and the roof.
I'll flick it through the gap.
So I started out towards it

stretching out with the toilet brush.
Nothing hurried.
Nice and easy.
Don't want it to jump off the wall at me.
'Course I'm not scared.
I'm doing it, aren't I?'
Then I reached it with the end of the toilet brush
and
flick!
That got rid of it.
Over the top of the wall.
Brilliant.
I'd got rid of the spider.

Then I looked down at the brush.
There it was.
Crawling up the handle of the brush
towards my hand.
'YAAAAAAAAAAAAAAAAA.
GET OFF, GET OFF, GET OFF.'
I shook the brush like mad.
That got rid of it.
Phew. I don't want to be bothered like that again.

Then my son Joe says,
'Dad.'
'Mmmm'
'Look at your foot.'
'What's the matter with it?'
I look down,

it's sitting there on my bare foot:
'YAAAAAAAAAAAAAAAAA.
GET OFF, GET OFF, GET OFF.'
Shake shake shake.
That got rid of it.

Course I wasn't scared of it.

The next night
we were sitting round having tea
and my Eddie (now 7 years old)
walks in from outside in his bare feet.
'Dad, Dad, quick over here.
There's a scorpion over here.'
Now you know what scorpions are, don't you?
Little land lobsters
with a tail that's a sting
that curls right over from the back
and wobbles about in front of them
zing, zing, zing.
And they've got two big nippers
that go
slicey, slicey, slicey.
I said, 'Don't be silly, Eddie,
they don't have scorpions in Australia.
Do you think we would let you walk about
in bare feet if we knew there were scorpions here?
You could tread on one of those
and next thing you know
it stings you

and your foot is swelling up like a football
vvvvoooooooh.
Or even worse:
you could sit on one of those things
and:
vvvvoooooooh.
You'd know about it, believe me.'
'Dad, it's a scorpion. Come over here and look.'
I said, 'I don't know what it is,
but it's not a scorpion, OK?
They're unbelievably dangerous.
One foot on one of those and –
vvvvoooooooh.'
'Dad. Listen to what I'm saying.
It's a scorpion.'
I said,
'OK, I'll come and have a look
but it won't be a scorpion, OK?'
I went over to have a look.

'Stand back everybody.
That is really dangerous.
THAT IS A SCORPION.'

'Yeah, that's what I was trying to tell you, Dad.'

'Nobody go anywhere near it.'
And I looked round for the biggest thing I could find.

It turned out to be
Richard Scarry's *Giantest Book Ever Ever*.
I lifted it up above my head and
blam!
Right on it.
And little bits of scorpion
went flying off in all directions.
That wasn't very Green of me, was it?
Probably wrecked the food chain in the area
for hundreds of years.
Anyway
I swept the bits of scorpion out
and I said to Eddie,
'Lucky you didn't tread on that.
One foot on it and
vvvvoooooooh.'
And he's nodding at me,
not saying anything.

Next day
he comes up to me and says,
'You know that scorpion yesterday?'
'Yep.'
'I did tread on it.'
'You trod on that scorpion?
Yesterday?
Why didn't you tell me at the time?'
And he shrugged his shoulders
and said all indignant:
'Dunnooooo'

'What do you mean, you don't know?'
'Dunnooo I dunnoooooo.'

And I've never found out
why he didn't tell me he trod on a scorpion.
Why couldn't he have said,
'Er Dad, I've trod on a scorpion.'?

One day Joe went to the shower.
He came running out of the shower.
He was pointing back at the shower
without saying anything.
I went over and had a look.
In the corner of the shower
on the ground was this thing.
A fat grey snake-thing with legs.
When it saw me
it opened its mouth.
And it was a huge mouth
like a little crocodile
except the mouth inside was bright red
and in the middle of the mouth
was a little blue tongue that waggled to and fro
like it was saying,
'*Don't you come in here or I'll bite your leg off.*'
I said to it,
'It's OK, we won't come in here.
Relax. The shower's all yours.'
When I turned round to leave
I brushed up against the shower curtain

and this one-foot-long stick insect
flew into my face.
It felt like a flying hand coming for me.
'Don't worry about them,'
my Australian friends said
when we got back to the city,
'they're nothing to worry about.'
'But what about the horse flies?' I said.
Like old Second World War bombers
looming up towards you
dzzzzzzzzzzzzzzzzzzzz,
hairy bodies, bright green eyes
and a little sharp triangle that they dig into your skin.

'Don't worry about *them*,' they said.
'Lucky you didn't see a Red Back.'
'A Red Back,' I said, 'what's a Red Back?'
'Oh it's just a little spider with a Red Back.'
'And what does it do?'
'Bites yer.
and – er – kills yer.'
'You don't see many of them around do you?' I said.
'Oh yeah, they're everywhere.
They love outside toilets and
little old houses in the bush.
You just brush your hands across one of them
and you know about it.
A few people die of them every year in Australia, you know.'
'Oh really?' I said, 'and what about those giant
grey furry spiders?

They're pretty dangerous too, aren't they?'
'Nope. Totally harmless, mate.
You can kiss them goodnight every night.
It's the little Red Back you want to watch out for.'
I felt all kind of weak.
Our little old house and our outside toilet
out there in the bush
were probably teeming with Red Backs.
They were probably in the bed.
And nobody told us.
We could all have been bitten to death
by hundreds of raving Red Backs.
All seven of us,
wiped out,
just like that.
And we never knew.

Eddie and the Car

The stupidest thing I have ever done
happened in France.
We were going to have a picnic,
so we were driving along the road
in our little yellow Renault 4
Have you ever seen a Renault 4?
It's like a square tin box.
If you lean on it, the walls are so thin
your hand goes straight through the side of the car.

We were off to have a picnic,
Have you noticed how long it takes
parents to make up their minds where to stop for a picnic?
It takes us longer to find where to have the picnic
than it takes to eat it.
We stop, we get out, we spread the sheet
we unload the boxes and bags and bottles
we sit down and it's
sniff
sniff
sniff
what's that?
what on earth could smell like that?
a dead dog?
OK
EVERYONE BACK IN THE CAR.

Drive on.

We stop, we get out, we spread the sheet
we unload the boxes and bags and bottles
we sit down and it's
zzzzzzz
zzzzzzz
zzzzzzz
wasps.
Hundreds of them.
OK
EVERYONE BACK IN THE CAR.

Drive on.

In the end we got to this perfect place.
Backed the car up a little slope
laid everything out on the ground
sat down.

'Eddie, do you want some chicken?'
'Na.'
'Eddie, do you want some crisps?'
'Na.'
'A drink?'
'Na.'
'Right, well, you toddle off
and leave us to eat in peace.'

So Eddie (who was three at the time)
walked off to the car
and he got into the back seat.
He looked out the window
and called out:
'Look at mee-eeeee.
I'm in the car.'
Joe, who was seven,
looks over and starts giggling back at Eddie.
'Look at Eddie, Dad,' says Joe.
'Turn round, Joe. Don't take any notice of him.
It only encourages him.
Turn round.'

Then Eddie climbed into the front seat of the car.
He grabbed hold of the steering wheel
and shouted out at us:
'LOOK AT ME-EEEEEE,
I'M DRI-VING.'
And Joe says,
'Look at Eddie, Dad
he's driving.'
I say,
'Turn round Joe,
don't take any notice of him.
It only encourages him.
Turn round.'

We went on eating.

Then Joe looked up and said,
'Dad.
The car's moving.'
I said, 'Don't be silly, Joe,'
and I turned round to look at the car.

He was right.
The car was moving slowly down the slope
towards the road
with Eddie at the wheel.
He is screaming:
'THE CAR'S MOVING. THE CAR'S
MOVING.'

Now if you were a sensible, intelligent person
at this moment
you might perhaps go over to the car
open the door
get Eddie out
jump in
jam on the brakes
and stop the car.

That would be the sensible thing to do.

Slightly less sensible
but still quite sensible
would be to
go over to the car
open the door
get Eddie out
close the door
and wave goodbye to the car.

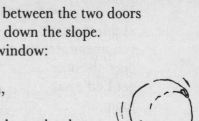

At least Eddie would be safe.

What I did was
try to stop the car.
I rushed over
and grabbed hold of the pillar between the two doors
and tried to stop the car going down the slope.
Eddie was screaming out the window:
'THE CAR'S MOVING!'
And I'm grunting back at him,
'I know it's moving.'
All the time the car is moving down the slope
and I'm hanging on.

On the roof of the car is a tray of peaches
so Joe is calling out,
'Dad, look at the peaches.
The peaches are flying off the roof of the car.'
and I'm saying, 'Never mind the peaches,'
And Eddie is shouting,
'The car's moving.'
'I know it's moving.'

Now I know that what we've got coming up next
is the road.
So I think, it'll be flatter there.
The car will slow down.
I'll be able to stop the car.
We get to the road.
The car doesn't slow down.
I am not able to stop the car.
'Dad, look at the peaches.'
'Never mind the peaches.'
'The car's moving.'
'I know it's moving.'

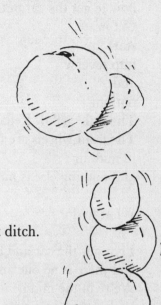

We are now heading for a twelvefoot ditch.

The car nosedives down the ditch
with me still hanging on.
It bounces once, twice on its nose
and lands up stuck head first in a hedge
with its wheels spinning in mid-air.

I opened the door, grabbed hold of Eddie
got him out
and he jumped into his mother's arms
and bit her.
He sunk his teeth right into her arm.
Joe is walking around saying,
'Look at the peaches
look at the peaches.'

Eddie is OK
now to get the car out of the hedge.
Get in
start up
into reverse
and
nothing.
The little yellow Renault 4 has front-wheel drive.
The front wheels are turning over and over
in mid-air
and nothing else is moving.

What to do?

I got out the car and looked round
and there is no one anywhere.
We're in the middle of the French countryside.
We're stuck in a hedge
miles from home.

Then I looked again
up the road
and I could see in a field
someone's backside.
A man was bending down
digging potatoes.
So I ran up the road and spoke to him.
'*Excusez-moi, monsieur,*
je suis Anglais et je suis stupide.
(I'm English and I'm stupid)
and my little boy got on the front seat of the car
and the car went down the hill
and
BLUP
it's stuck.'

The man stood up
and slowly wagged his finger at me.
'*Jamais, jamais, jamais* –
(Never, never, never)
Never let a child on to the front seat of a car
they can easily –'
'Yeah I know that *now*,' I said,
'but how do I get the car out?'
He then raised both hands by his side and said,
'*Bof*!'
This is French for:
'I haven't got a clue
you're on your own, mate.'

Try it:
raise both arms
by your side
hands upwards
and as you say it
puff your cheeks out:
'Bof!'

So now what?

Far away in the distance
I see a man ploughing a field
so I started off running up the road
towards him.
As I am running along
I start to realize that I am only wearing my underpants.
When we had the picnic
I thought I would sunbathe.
So here I am running down the road
in my underpants.
No matter.

Must press on.

As I got nearer to the field
where the man was ploughing
I started thinking,
how *do* you get someone to stop ploughing a field?

So I climbed over the fence
and stood in front of the tractor

held up both my hands
and started waving.
I don't suppose the farmer
had ever seen a large hairy bloke
in his underpants
standing in front of his tractor waving his hands.
But he brought the tractor up to me and stopped it.
And he said,
'*Hé bien?*'
which is French for:
'Well? Have you got something to say or not?
Or are you completely stupid?'
As you say it you have to nod your head upwards
leaving your mouth open after you've said it.
The 'bien' bit sounds like 'bang' said through your nose.
Try it.

So I said,
'*Excusez-moi, monsieur,*
je suis Anglais et je suis stupide.
(I'm English and I'm stupid)
and my little boy got on the front seat of the car
and the car went down the hill
and
BLUP
it's stuck.'

The man looked at me
and slowly wagged his finger at me and said
'*Jamais, jamais, jamais,*'
(Never, never, never)
let a child get into the front seat of a car
because they can easily –
'Yeah, yeah, yeah, I know that *now*
but do you think you could help me?
I could pay you . . .
it would be very nice if . . .'

So three hours later
after he had lunch
he came along with his tractor
his wife
his dog
and a long chain.
They tied the chain round the back bumper of the car
and they pulled and they heaved
and they heaved and they pulled
(just like the story of The Enormous Turnip)
and they pulled and they heaved the bumper
right off the car.

Thanks.

Well, in the end
they got the little yellow Renault 4 out of the bush
and out of the ditch.
After we had kicked it a few times
it worked.
It was a bit difficult going round corners
but it worked.
We've got a photo of the
little yellow Renault 4
stuck in the ditch
in our photo album.
It's great.
It reminds me of
the stupidest thing I have ever done.

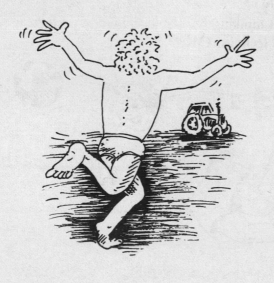

Mr Baggs

I was walking home from school
with Mr Baggs
the teacher who took us for football
and he said:
'You see Michael, what we need in the team
is a really good centre-half,
someone who can control the game from midfield
collect the ball in the middle
distribute the ball to the front players.
A good centre-half can turn a game.
He can make all the difference.
Now who have we got playing in the middle?
– oh, my goodness it's you
I forgot
I'm sorry
I wasn't thinking
no hard feelings, O K?'

My Friend Roger

My friend Roger says
that I can't walk up the road with him
in case his parents see me
so I say goodbye to him
at the corner of the road.

But sometimes I just
lean
round
the edge
of the wall on the corner
and watch him walk up the road
on his own.

Mum's School

My mum is a teacher
and once she had to take me to school with her.
Her children lined up in the playground
ready for games.
I was at the back.
It was all quiet,
we were waiting to begin.

I looked up
and then I skipped round to the front of the line
in a great big circle
round to the front
round to the back
skip skip skip.

Then Graham thought he would do the same
and he started to skip round
round to the front
round to the back
skip skip –
but my mum sent us in.

We sat in the classroom
and Graham taught me
Inky pinky ponky,
the farmer bought a donkey,
the donkey died,
the farmer cried,
inky pinky ponky.

That night at home
Mum said that I had let her down
and it made her sad
what was I trying to do?
show her up in front of her children?
well?
what have you got to say for yourself?
well?

and I didn't say anything
I just looked at the floor
feeling hot

well? she said
and I said
er –
inky pinky ponky.

107

The Cupboard

At the top of the stairs
there's a landing
that's where the bedrooms are
our bedroom
and Mum and Dad's bedroom.

At the top of the stairs
there's a landing
that's where the bedrooms are
our bedroom
and Mum and Dad's bedroom
and the cupboard.

The walk-in cupboard
with no floor at the back
where the walls slope down
with the roof of the house
down to narrow grey corners.

The walk-in cupboard
with no light
where the old brown metal trunk
and the old grey metal trunk
stand on end
tall and empty
like caves
that would welcome you in
and shut tight behind you.

The walk-in cupboard
where two gas-masks
lie between the timbers
like crazy skulls
and Dad's army jacket talks of tanks
and dead heads.

The walk-in cupboard
where my brother showed me
behind the trunks
was a little low door
leading into a lightless nothing
where
with a wriggle
he said you could get through
– go on
and I did
and once in,
there was nothing
and nothing
and nothing
until
my head hit a box.

A slit of light leaked through a slipped slate
in the roof.
I opened the box
it was stacked to the top
with sheets of paper
written on
letters to Mum from Dad
when he was away
as the war was ending
when my brother was small
and he was coming home
and he was leaving home
and he was coming home
just before I was born.

Pneumonia

My brother has pneumonia
and the house is quiet.

I am allowed in his room
FOR A SHORT TIME ONLY.

My brother has pneumonia
and the house is quiet.

When I go in he shows me
a little row of glass bottles with rubber lids
that go pop pop pop pop pop

he shows me a tiny cardboard locomotive he's made
and we go digger de doo, digger de doo

I sit on his bed and – whoofff
and I spill his orange juice on his blanket

Mum comes in and says
Get out get out, look what you've done.

My brother has pneumonia
and the house is quiet.

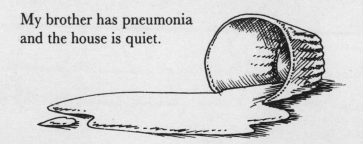

Sweetshop

do you think there's a sweetshop here?
are we going to the sweetshop?
when are we going to the sweetshop?
will you take me to the sweetshop?
have we got enough money for the sweetshop?
will the sweets be in jars in the sweetshop?
will they have homemade sweets in the sweetshop?
will they have those soft squashy toffees with the chocolate
inside
in the sweetshop?
are we going to the sweetshop?
when are we going to the sweetshop?
will you take me to the sweetshop?
have we got enough money for the sweetshop?
will you take me to the sweetshop?
when are we going to the sweetshop?
are we going to the sweetshop?
are we?

For Naomi

I'm the kind of dad
my children don't want to be seen with
because I'm the kind of dad who

shouts in shops
says hello to babies
doesn't clean the car
eats pizzas in the street
doesn't cut his moustache
sings on buses
argues with policemen
waves to old ladies
has long hair
and
writes poems

Three-Year-Old Boy Says:

I can't catch the air
I want to catch the air
and dump it all in my mouth

My pasta is kidnapped
and my mouth is a dungeon

O look at the cat
her skin is bursting
through her fur.

Does she know she's a cat?

Is a sheepdog a half-dog, half-sheep?

I hate you, Bear-poo

I like Coughed Wheat

I can't go to my party because I haven't got an invitation.

You wait till I'm older than you!

Conversation With a Six-Year-Old

Do you want to come to my party?
Yes.
You'll get ice-cream jelly
a punch in the belly
you can't watch telly
cos your feet are too smelly.
Thanks.

Proverbs

On the wall in our house
we've got a picture called 'Flemish Proverbs'.

There are hundreds and hundreds of people in it
acting out different proverbs and fables like
'It's no use crying over spilt milk.'
'Big fish eat little fish.'
and the story of the fox and the stork.

There are ones we don't have like
one about someone trying to tile his roof with pies
and one about someone trying to cut wool off a pig.

The picture is full of kings and hats and snakes and fires
and rivers and knights in armour
all in one huge picture
on our front room wall.

My friends come over and look at it.

They come to look at the rude bits.

There's an inn-sign of a moon
and there's a man looking out of the window
peeing on it.
The proverb is about a show-off –
'He thinks he's so clever, he can pee on the moon.'

There's one where all the men have got their trousers off
and they're bending down
walking backwards into a little house.
The proverb is about several people trying to do
something
that only one person can do.
'They think they can all do a poo in the same toilet.'

My friends have got pictures in their houses:
'Elephants at Dawn'
and
'Brixham Harbour'.
I quite like them
but they say,
'Let's go over to Michael's place
and look at the rude bits on his parents' picture.'

Shirt

Whenever my mum gets me some horrible shirt
that I don't want to wear
she says,
'It's good. Have it. It's nice.
They're wearing them like that now.'

So I wear it to school.

And whenever I come home from school
she says,
'So? Did they like the shirt?'

Sometimes I go off a favourite food
and my mum says,
'What's the matter with him?
He used to love apricot jam.
Why don't you want the apricot jam?
I got it in specially for you.
You said you liked it.
So I bought it.
You've always liked apricot jam.
I can remember a time
when the only thing you would have on your bread
was apricot jam
and now you're telling me you don't like it?
It's good. Have it. It's nice.'

So I have the apricot jam.

And when I have eaten it
she says,
'So? Did you like the apricot jam?'

Found Poem: Safety Instructions on United Airlines 1995

'If you are sitting in an exit row
and you cannot understand this card
or cannot see well enough
to follow these instructions
please tell a crew member.'

I thought:
But if I can't understand the card
how can I understand it
to tell someone I can't understand it?

Invisible Ink

Dad?
Yup.
What can you use for invisible ink?
Lemon juice.

(I get lemon juice,
matchstick,
piece of paper,
I write something.)

Dad?
Yup.
I can't read it.

Index of First Lines